SHIVER

SHIVER

Lynn Martin

Tender Buttons Press
New York City
www.TenderButtonsPress.com

Tender Buttons Press
New York City
www.TenderButtonsPress.com

Contents

Shiver

Carolina Handler

Sundays, I dance with the snake –
she coils in my arms and her
copper head, like a new penny,
weaves as I sway to the music.
And this is how I pray.
And this is how I pray.
Her warm long belly slides
knowing, now, another skin – not
rock or root or clay, but I
am as solid. I resonate.
Flick of the tongue and
she has my scent. We
were never strangers anyway.
We wind like the wild
grapevine – embracing Eden.
When eye to red-eye and
fearlessly we meet,
I am as teeming as
the spring-fed pond.
I am lighter than
a skipping stone.
I am a sacred woman –

a copper bangled woman.
My bracelets are alive.
And "I'm coming up.
I'm coming up on
the rough side of the mountain."
Here is the flame of tongue.
Again and again the tongue
stuttering as we writhe.
In another language I pray.
In another language I pray.
Then slowly ever so
slowly we uncoil and
holy Jesus on Sunday
evening sets us free.

Now, there are clouds on the mountains.
I stand where the earth is red.

Deadfish/Rockfish

"I went to Florida once,"
my friend Jimmy Harris says.
Then he spits on the ground.

It is almost summer.
The good news is honeysuckle.
And we are standing on
the gravel road – our battered
pickups, parked and pointed
in opposite directions.

"I went swimming in the ocean –
salt water. And when I came
out of that water, my skin
was so salty and dry,"
here he spits again,
"I felt like a dead fish."

And here we live
in a blue mountain hollow
beside a spring-fed creek
where not a mile down the road

runs a river – clear and clean
called "Rockfish."
Or, simply, the river.
Or even more simply, home.

Seeds

Life attacks life without hatred.
                                    —Rilke

Amazing. How quick the grass sprouts
along the newly carved road.
How the green hairs of rye
work to hold the banks.

Once, in Mexico, I stayed
with an old friend. In
her kitchen, she argued
with a scorpion. It ran
from the boom of her voice.
But the silence between threats
rendered the little stinger
bold enough to march back –
stamping its many legs.

One ant, burdened by a seed on its back,
stops to rest – kneeling in the red dust.

No Difference on
Old Roberts Mountain

Wind whisks through
this one-room shack.
Hard rain and the roof leaks.
No difference between outside
and in. Either way through
the rippled window glass
moss and wood, humming
insects, rash birdsong.

Chinking the Cabin

1

Picture this:
hand-made homestead
planted on the rise
two hundred years ago.
The chestnut logs –
broad and long,
raised and stacked,
square and plumb.
Two hundred years
standing level and true.

But between the logs
spaces, once chinked
with horsehair and mud,
wink or gape open
to call in sun, rain,
frigid winds and in spring
the sparrow her nest
above the doorway.
In the darkest corner
a black snake winters
then lays her eggs.

2

I learn the recipe
from a restoration expert.
I climb the ladder
with a bucketful of mix.

3

I begin on the north side
where the house has weathered most.
Ask the hornets and
mud daubers to kindly move on.
And they listen and they do
with sweet electric drone.

4

You must think like rain, she said.
So with my trowel between logs,
I bevel the quick-setting mix
    deep above
        shallow below.
So the earthbound rain will flow.

5

Now picture this:
For two hundred years –
a cabin, planted on the rise,
with all the lamps lit.
And whenever you arrive,
there's someone standing
in the doorway, looking out.

Now, in Late October, I Can See

In late October, I can see
the mountain; the little lights.
I see the last of the sun's glow
through the hollow, across the creek
where thick groves of golden
poplar answer almost as brightly.
And to the west, the mountain
strewn with lights – a city
built on rock where the twisted trees
have so much to say about the wind.

On the path which is nearly dark,
I am looking for a turtle shell.
Last year I found one here in the leaves –
a bleached abandoned vehicle.
Do you know the old story about creation?
How the swimming turtle offered
its shell for the world?
Buoyant and balanced, turtle paddled,
and, listen, still paddles
skimming the surface of infinity.

This world is an island.
A cloud-capped floating dome
where the first woman, who fell
like a leaf from the sky,
gently landed on her feet,
then stepped, ever so lightly,
into the deep, tranquil woods.
Some say she followed a bear – walking
erect, like a beautiful man, to his den.
Together, they peopled Turtle Island.

From here, in late October,
on the tilting ground of the world,
I look toward the falling sun and see
the crowded mountain – where street lights
and house lights burn long
before night, that old friend, comes in.
Where the black bear finds
nothing familiar, except, sometimes,
the weather – the high, howling wind,
and a few trees bent on living.

I remember how, once, I felt
the ground quake – the turtle tossing,
and I fell on hands and knees
just to hold on. The path
is darker now. The leaves are damp
and deep. And I am on my knees again.
Surely this is a kind of prayer –
looking for a turtle shell – this relic
beneath so many fallen leaves.

Shiver

It's winter in this
gap-toothed hollow
where sun and sparrow
are swallowed whole.

A woman lies down,
makes mountains with her body,
gives me her tongue –
wing beat and spark.

And I cling with many fingers
like honeysuckle to rock
rooted to the earth
of this desire.

Lonesome Mountain Hullabaloo

Reckon this mountain's the ear of the world.
Hear highway traffic and freight train moan,
birdsong, salsa music, one violin.
Now the whir of a small plane's propeller.
Now braggadocio rooster crows.
Even on Lonesome, a hullabaloo.
Wind-flexed limbs of hillside hemlock, dry beech
leaves like surf, long needled pines rub creaking.
As woodpeckers knock the weakest trees, listen.
Deep in the woods, beside the trickling creek,
someone; who is it? Who murmurs and weeps?
Deer bark warning and stamp delicate hooves.
Then the axe cleaving a round of red oak.
Then pale echoes of that dividing stroke.

Heaven

Seven doe bounding up the snowy mountain.
The last glances back, glances back at
her spike – young buck, like a tentative
shepherd, who follows the blazed trail.

Snowbound, on the mountain, with seven lines.
To climb out of shadow into light, tell yourself
syllables will follow – hoof prints on the snowy path.

From deep hollow to sun-glazed mountaintop,
deer ascend and, to the naked eye, blasted
by light, transcend this ordinary world.

Potomac

A faint voice from the riverside
cries out like a child's –
high pitched. So you move to it.

Another scream urges you
deeper into the suburban woods
while your heart utters prayers.

And following the cries
to the water's edge, you see
the fox – fastened to the wide-eyed fawn.

Turning away is that old grinding circle.
All afternoon the fawn will
call to you from the river,
"Alive! Alive!"

Mounds

In this place
       Everywhere.
We are walking on bones:
oak, rabbit skull, wing.
Here the bones of my ancestors
       lie in these woods
     marked by mounds of stone.

See, a tree has rooted
     in someone's heart.

Woodwork

After so many years, you learned
the nature of the work.
When this was all you could have:
scorched heart pine – tongue and
groove. Abandoned, oak barn boards.
Sweet scented, blood-red cedar.

Once a builder told me this story.
A man came looking for work.
He had a hammer and a rusty
hand-saw. It was a local job –
sidewalks for the neighborhood.
Simple form work to hold the mix
until the concrete set hard.

Backwoods, fresh milled poplar.
Chestnut. Walnut – stacked and
drying for a hundred years in
someone's catch-all shed.

So the builder gave the man
dimensions, a pile of boards, a bucket
of nails. Then the builder kindly
walked away. Said he'd be back.
The man kneeled. Leaned into his saw.

When this was all you could have:
warehouse pallets, railroad ties,
scorched heart pine, green
falling-into-the-river birch.

"Now imagine," said the builder, "finding
a form so perfectly joined, you could
take it home and live with it
like a well-made thing."

Scorched heart pine. Green
falling-into-the-river birch.

Needing 29 Windows and Looking for a Break, I Went to the Factory in Rocky Mount

All along the road felt like home.
Winding. Red earth. Green trees. Fields
of fresh-cut hay and young yellow corn.
Old, yawning houses – window panes
of rippled glass. Rivers and woods. Then
a man-made blue mountain lake.
Motor boats. Real estate.

I stopped for a smoke at a national park –
and walked to the birthplace of Booker T.
Slave's quarters. A reconstructed hovel.
Dirt floors. Then I saw a film of his life.
How it was. A child hauling water.
Weeding crops. When he was a man and
free, he built a university –
brick by home-made ruddy brick.
Because knowledge takes work. Is a body's ambition.

Once his mother stole a chicken.
In the middle of the night she woke her children,
and they ate like hungry possums.
Because to eat is a body's ambition, too.

Train tracks through the factory town.
Train tracks through old Rocky Mount.
With two factories for the square and the round
windows. Windows. Windows.

He was a very old man. He said he retired
but the bosses asked him back
to manage the seconds – overstocks, scratched
and dented. At least he was out
of that factory, he said, and I heard his grief
sharp as the screech of branches against panes.

In the windowless warehouse, we shifted stock.
And because I had specifications, we found
only one window to fit the house I was building.
So I saved forty dollars and the old man's tired back.

Train tracks through the factory town.
Train tracks through sad Rocky Mount.
Saved forty dollars and the old man's back.
Saved forty dollars and the old man's back.

Ghosts

If everyone's on computers,
who's gonna do the work?
−Jimmy Harris

When Jimmy Harris leans in close,
you smell woodsmoke, hay, and motoroil.

Over his shoulder, in the yard, you can
see lilacs and chickens and swinging
from the clothesline, five pair of green
coveralls − like ghosts dancing
in the breeze and dappled sunlight.

So when Jimmy Harris, fully embodied
and cradling a giant wrench, bows
beneath the old truck's battered hood,
how you relish the sure scent of him.

There's a pine grove edging the yard
and beyond all this, a pale blue mist
clings to the side of a distant mountain.

Red Oak and Pine

Logging truck
rolls down the road
with red oak and pine –
bodies stacked high.

Sap flows
long after the whine
of the saw has died.

Freshly severed,
in the iron stove –
hear the hiss and moan
of red oak.

Let us sit and honor
so many lives –
our tables, our chairs,
this house made of wood.

Vixen

I stumble
into the snow shovel.
It slides down
the wall – tin
against clapboard makes
that quick metallic shriek.

A fox barks back.
It is a love call
in the dark; my hair
stands up. It's
spring and now I
am a vixen and
this is my den.
Come in. Come in.

Today the Flowers

Today the flowers
are anesthesia.
I see reds and yellows.

Now the trees
are white dogs
with sweet breath.

Now the birds
perch and confess.
But I am guilty.

I forget the world
of tender constructions.
I forget the world
of houses and hearts.

Skyfish

Now here's the moon – skyfish
leaping over great cloud foam.

I'm home from working the evening
shift, in early spring, after a rain.

Mist, thick as cream, pools
in the deep cups of the hollows.

Along the edge of the field among
sharp, glistening pines, I see wild

apple blossoms shimmer like pearls.
And I want to wake all you sleepers,

even the children. Here is a rainbarrel.
Where spawning constellations rise

to the brimful surface, now
a nimble spider casts her net –

a perfect mesh. O my phosphorescent.
My blue gilled heart.

And sometimes the moon

is a woman in her kitchen
stirring the starry soup
as one buttery crescent
rises in the oven.
Then, no matter who you are,
you can sit at her table.
You can drink this wine.
When no matter who you are,
if you look and look,
she looks back.

Union Poem

Isn't it true, as the sparrow
knows its song, we have
always known our beloved's?
The taste of those paradisal notes?
Didn't we always live there –
in verdant hills beside the sea?
Only now do we whole-
heartedly embrace this truth.
Only now, when we kiss,
does memory of this melody
spark and flame. Yes.
Isn't it true? Like the sparrow
on fire – singing in the thicket.
we have always been and
will be in the thick of it.

Heartwood

Notice how the hand cradles those tools with handles
hewn from heartwood. How the arc of an ax or a hammer
is a signature. Here to there, back and forth, notice the wind
in the scythe, the sickle, the weaver's shuttle; how
from smooth grain and a knot of muscle, comes the steady
hiss and crack and hum of this one endless life.

Laborers

for Jean Vallon

In Boston, we gutted old buildings
for landlords and speculators; plowing
knee-deep through plaster and debris.
Then, quickly quickly, making rooms whole
again. New walls. Fresh paint. Polished
floors. So it was a kind of living.
We worked hard, paid our bills and
after this, when we had just potatoes
and government cheese to eat –
five-pound blocks of cheddar – gifted
by poor friends on the dole, I baked
deep-dish casseroles and they were good.
Then we laughed at hunger. Then
we practiced the art of it.

We danced to our neighbor's booming salsa.
They, wisely, raised chickens in the empty lot.
Our slumlord was a Catholic priest.
He had no guilt. This is the truth.
I wrapped socks around the toilet seat

for insulation; it was so cold.
A few blocks away, on a sidewalk
in the better neighborhood, I found
a sleeper sofa discarded with the trash.
So I rolled it down to our place.
Sold it for thirty dollars. Then we ate
something else.

In America, this is the truth,
the harder you work, the less you're paid.
We ate potatoes and cheddar by the five-pound block.
I found a sofa. Sold it. Then we ate something else.

Appalachian Dolphins

I dream of two dolphins –
one and then the other
curled like question marks,
sleek and pale, they leap
above the surface
of my mountain-fed, ever
connecting rivers and it's
puzzling. What does this
mean? I must tell someone –
a climatologist or shaman.
Or find a bodega dream book
and play the lottery numbers
for river dolphin dreams. How
happy they seem – immigrants
so at ease, these two verge
downstream – rise and dive,
flashing bonny smiles, splashing
in and out of the green torrent.
Yes, I must tell someone.

"Earth Felt the Wound"

–Milton, *Paradise Lost*, Book Nine

Let the dog without a friend, the one
with the mange-disfigured face, running
through the deep, rusted leaves, leaping
over downfallen limbs, the one haunted
by burrs and loneliness, who pauses
at the edge of the wood, who pauses
to look at you, let this cast-off coy
dog find a fresh, sinewy bone.
Let the songbirds sing on.
Let earth not look away.

Now's the Rapture

One of a kind – this oil stick painting –
the roller skater takes a bow;
a red stitched cardinal in a tiny frame;
the twisted tree beneath a strange sky.

One of a kindness – the leaflike
arrowhead misses its mark. Only
now, you notice it, a thousand years later
when earth gives it up.

Look, this bliss, this improvised
life's all you've got to go on.
Build your heart muscle – push
your stone loaded cart through mud.
Then empty it.

Let's Talk About Nature and Truth

Picture this.
You live in Peekskill, New York.
You own a Chevy Malibu.
Say its painted candy-apple red.
In the evening, after work
you park it in the driveway;
polish the hubcaps
till they gleam.

Night falls. You're inside
watching the local news.
So you don't see the celestial
dazzle, the streak, the blaze.
But you hear that meteor
slam like a bomb
into the trunk of your car –
parked in your driveway
in Peekskill, New York.

Here's another true story:
At the edge of the field,
during the ice storm,
an old dogwood snaps.
And the rootless crown
comes to a shattering rest –
angled among icicled brambles ...

But get this: in spring it
blossoms yet
like a bride's veil
so white and,
now the thick of it,
dazzling in the dark.

Too Much Sky

"I used to look up to the mountain,
but now I look down," said
the saddest man in West Virginia –
where logging trucks, then massive
dump trucks, spewing diesel smoke,
haul away our precious cargo – old wind
twisted trees, the wild laurel, the flame
azalea, vines, tiny white flowers, mosses,
earth carved from the mountaintop,
boulder, root and bone. Then deeper.
Deeper than the deepest worm.
Shattered rock of ages.
Now this is how we mine the coal.
Where once a mountain, now a hole.
And there's too much sky.

Mockingbird Variations

Glory! Glory! Glory!
Your voice – my pulse.
So ruffle some feathers
then worry the line.
Do what you have to do.
From the tallest treetop,
among speechless stars,
you're lord of the world
laying down the law:
Come union come union
communion communion come
glory glory glory!

Stalin's Daughter

I'm a kind of prisoner in small-town Wisconsin –
where there's always a cricket in the public library
trilling like a scholar; where grief can take a solitary
amble down a long, lonesome road. And so
knee-deep in these almost Siberian winters,
I listen. Listen for spring's migration songs.
For who does not love the birds? ... the robin and the lark?
Even this congress of dark, roosting vultures – wing beat
like soft thunder, lifting as one from the snowbound pine?

Revolution

This poem's a fish on its belly
crawling out of the pond.
Who would believe it?
Just when you thought you'd seen it all,
something like this happens. Look,
this fish can go anywhere.

Excerpts from the Memoirs
of a Lavatory Attendant

for Virginia Woolf

Once I had a lover
with a fetish for uniforms –
delivery driver, cop, soldier,
but not this sack of drab
which says, I wipe the counters,
mop the floors, which says,
I am the alchemist of disinfectants.
I keep it clean.

· · ·

Earthbound snow like ashes.
Not code for god or grief.
Just this particular snowfall.

· · ·

Do not think I was born for this.
That my mother looked into my infant eyes
and said, "This one will clean the toilet."
No. But, like dogs, some of us are pampered,
others short-chained to a tree in the yard,
our battered buckets and bowls upturned.

Astonished the Trees

Astonished the poplars are in love and cannot hide it.
Sap rises, leaves unwind. Everywhere, day by day,
by and by, another flower – another delicate body opens.
Their petals, fluent tongues, astonished the trees say it.

Black Bear by Minnie Adkins

Mostly mouth, each tooth carefully carved
and between these teeth, lolls the tongue.

In eastern Kentucky, seeking grubs,
hunger lumbers through the wooded world –
she who leaves no mossy stone unturned.

She who plucks the bee-stung blackberry –
red tongue, white teeth, fierce grin.

Yesterday I Went into the Woods

Yesterday I went into the woods
but could not hear the insect
or birdsong. I could not hear
the wind bending the trees and
how ten-thousand tender leaves
turned and turned again.
No. I reeled, my friend, and heard
only this – my clinging, keening mind.
So I sat with it.
To be compassionate.

Today the insects roar. The mind
is quiet. It must have been the wind
that laid this one, red oak
down. It must have groaned
then snapped – thumping the ground
like the skin of a drum. I praise and
prune the leafy limbs. With gratitude
for the gushing of sparrows,
I cut, split and stack the wood.

The Next World

Walking home. It's near dusk.
There's a bend in the road
then red confetti,
because one almost naked maple
is celebrating the end of summer.
Little owls whistle and weep.
You see gay leaves, groundfall;
here's the green husk of a walnut –
the next world. And then
you see it coming –
the great trunk, nesting songbirds,
waving limbs, hosanna leaves.
You see it all in the moment
before night falls like a blindfold.

Departure

She says not, 'Goodbye,'
but 'Fare thee well.'
Late summer. 1962.
I'm almost five.
We stand beside
the cavernous sedan
idling in the street;
then look up, scan
the bruised sky.
She sighs – this sound
this unbidden out breath,
which my only mother
told me meant, *sad*.
But here she's glowing
as she sighs, then
Grandma utters another
new word, *sunset*
meaning the shock
of beauty and the riven.

After Sandy Hook

Take heart. Take heart, you workers
in the furrowed fields of love.
Try to trade bad thoughts for good.
Try to recall summer's creekside birdsong.
What a heavenly racket in that thicket –
a boisterous chorus, like twenty children at play.

Take heart. Take heart, all you workers.

Siren

First, the effervescent hiss
of surf. Then all at once comes
the glistening rubble – pebbles,
unstrung beads of coral and shell,
glass bits like petals, swollen
seeds scatter, bones clatter,
salt shaker. *All at once*
says the rasping sea.
All at once the sea.

Peligroso. They do not read the sign.
Dangerous. Rip-tide. Two swimmers,
pale as plaster statues, have arrived.
Young, reckless, foreigners,
they dash into the waves.
Peligroso. Dangerous. Rip-tide.

Beyond the breakers
brown pelicans hover,
hover then dive –

plunging into green waters.
Yellow bills, like spoons,
scoop up the little fishes.

A woman on her roof, pinning towels
and sheets to a line, calls out.
Her voice is a siren. The barefoot
builders lay down their trowels.
Children, then all the village women –
wringing their hands, come running.
Even the dogs, pausing now and
again to scratch their fleas,
join the gathering where two
pale swimmers entered the sea.

~~~~

Faultlines, canyons and plateaus.
Skeletal shipwrecks encrusted
with shellfish and sea moss.
Jutting, jagged, shattering rocks.
Blast of undulant sea trumpet.
The tidal whirl and suck.

"So there was the sea. We had
travelled far. The sun was hot;
the sand like walking on fire.
There was a seaside café with music
and free running chickens. Then,
all at once, there was only the sea."

~~~~

Deep inside the sodden hull
of the boat's wooden bow,
he was the child lulled to sleep
by the lapping sea and sloshing
buckets – thick with flopping fish
which topple and spill into dream.

He dreams the moon is rocking, rocking;
adrift like a boat on the horizon. Now
voices trill, "*peligroso peligroso*"
Startling. Children, like pipers,
peck and wake the fisherman.

And now he's seizing a coil of rope.
And now he's racing toward a chorus

of women, leaning seaward; they point there.
There! Two swimmers she wants to keep.
"Ay! Last night she was hissing;
her whispers like curses. So
I sang when my husband,
with his buckets of fish,
with his torn nets, came ashore.
But now the sea, oh terrible beauty!
See how she lures him back! I point
and shout, 'Peligroso!' I murmur,
'Bitter woman.' I spit on the sand."

He sees them in the eddies −
like driftwood, two swimmers purl.
So plunging into the swirl, he paddles
and skims the gritty, chopping swells −
where the current tears the water − a frayed
split open seam; where whipped waves collide,
break and boom. From this tormented
sea, the fisherman deftly delivers
one, and then the other pale swimmer.

"Ay! Now here's the other
one my swift husband saved.
I slap his pale face.
I shout, 'Peligroso!'
But this almost ghost just shrugs
and hands me a sopping wad of pesos,
as if a life is worth only this.
I pocket it. I spit on the sand.
As if our lives are worth just this."

Dust

Taking out a wall
of non-load-bearing plaster.
Dust everywhere in puffs.
Air laden with dust, you're
working in this neighborhood
near National Cathedral.
Or was it the time when
replacing that front porch
Georgian column, and a car
stopped on the shady street?
And so typically, there was
someone laying on the horn.
Don't look. Don't look.
You looked up.
when the driver, an older
 woman, yelled out the car window,
"All the power to you, honey!"

Somehow, was it on the radio?
You heard the Dalai Lama
was visiting the cathedral.
So you took a break, grabbed
a bodega coffee, and
wandered over to the steps
of that grand edifice
where a small crowd congregated.
Doors swing open. The exile exhales.
He's giggling and might as well be naked
among bishops ornate in drag.
And you were clutching your
coffee. And you were powdered
with dust. And why
were you crying, crying,
and why?

Come Winter

The window is a polished mirror
of my heart so lush.
I am rooted, evergreen.
I have delicate, spraylike foliage.
And here, a cluster of firm red berries.
Come winter, they will ripen.
They will taste so sweet.
I'll feed the little birds.
The juncos. The chickadees.

Shadows Winged By

Light. The snow-packed earth's a radiant canvas.
So what if the dream now is a tender prayer.
The sun, a glittering melody, pours through
the windows. It's all in your heart, you say,
blinded by awe and a kind of beggar's happiness.
And then, you see again, the face of your mother,
as once when birds and their shadows winged by,
that flicker of joy, that current of light –
subtle yet shocking, and she so desperately alive.
Now you tend to this vision, this prism –
shattered light all in your heart, you say.

Taste of Salt

Gull cry over the hilly streets of Brighton.
Rumble of Sussex-bound buses.
The varied little cafes and shops are closed
so early along this narrow, cobbled alleyway.
Seaside, smooth stones roll in and out.
Still ferris wheel at the end of the quay.
See wind-chopped swells, beached upturned
boats, fish heads, fog drift, this misty
light. A model poses for a photo shoot.
She stands astride a brand-new bike
as gulls cry and alight on steeples and
rooftop spires of sea-kissed Brighton.
Taste of salt on your lips.

Swannanoa

On Afton Mountain, empty fountains,
formally placed in the gardens
of this marble palace
in such disrepair, despair.
Nothing. Not a sip for the little birds.
The lion's face roars silence.
All the statues long gone. Once
towering above these green valleys,
where's Jesus now?
No gods in this forsaken place –
this tribute to what cannot abide.

A gentle wind. Clear winter day.
On the ground I find a plastic
lighter with a colorful design and
the words, *Knowledge is in your mind.*
Flick and miracle – a flame.

Wholly

for Dorian Stacy Brown

Impossible to forget this child
you have loved for twenty years.
You try to hold each other up, but
grief, this sea, wears you down.
And you want to know why
these wild flowers, rooted in stone,
wither and bloom, wither and bloom?
And why does this waning moon
now, red as coral, wholly come
back, come back?

Continental Drift

Androgynous defined
by a Connecticut ride,
you were that road
waif thumbing
with your back to traffic,
gliding from here to there,
driving time or better.

Sometimes you phone your mother.
Where are you?
She wants to know.

Dew drenched on a foggy mountaintop,
West Virginia. Wake up!
Birdsong. Wind in the wild laurel.

Thumbing with your back to traffic,
once you turned around to find a hearse –
ominous, waiting. And when the driver
saw your stunned, pale face,
he laughed. Then you laughed, too,
and took the ride.

Cattlemen and crop dusters.

In the desert, a sudden storm,
a vast violent sky,
and you were afraid.

Tell them,
"I'm from the Bronx."
Tell them,
"I carry a knife and
know how to use it."

Hard riding, independent truckers
tune into their cb radios,
high lonesome music,
and you to stay awake.

Cross country,
hauling to Baltimore,
but he took you to the Jersey Turnpike
Walt Whitman Rest Area
for just one
sweet kiss
on the lips
and that was all.

A breeze,
high dunes,
rabbits, coyote song,
starblast.

Where are you?
She wants to know.

John Elm,
Apache warrior,
rattling Thunderbird,
picked you up in Yuma
for a long beauty ride.

Scholars and sweating salesmen
with creeping hands.
A family says grace in a Winnebago.
Chicago rush hour roar.
The gusts take your hat
again and again until
you're weeping
this infernal evening
when, like the wind,
no one stops.

Adirondack blizzard.
Kicked out of a squeaky rig
stacked tight with dynamite
because you had no interest
in the driver's intimate tattoos.
Snow swirl.
Soft snow bank.
Your lover so near.

How many miles to the moon and back?

With your back to traffic?
With your little songs?
With your frayed, green canvas
boy scout pack?
Pickup trucks with gun racks,
an ambulance, Cadillacs.

Stillness in motion.
Undulant transcendence.
Cracked cup of spat tobacco
sloshes beside you on the seat.

Coal miners, lobstermen,
drag queens, waitresses
all full of grace.
Kindness and grace.
Radiant transport!

Where are you?

No Question

Take me to the Bay of Fundy.
Let's dare the racing tide
and stand upon a smooth rock
shelf about to be submerged.
Then we'll travel to the girlhood
village of Bishop to find
the farmhouse with its cavernous
barn attached to it.
We'll look up through the little
skylight in her child-sized room.
Little wonder she did not stay home.
Yes, happy she did not stay home.

Take me to the Bay of Fundy.
Let's dare the rising tide.

Pentimenti

You dream of arches, columns, narrow cobbled
alleyways, the wet whisper of Minerva.
This train you're on is dark and still.
Is it Bath? What century?

The counterfeit coin forged of iron
not bronze, found by a farmer along
the old Roman road still has the face
of an emperor. Such pleasure it gives you –
this old trick – what's rendered unto Caesar.

Now it all comes back. There the hillside
billboard of a chalk white horse. Neolithic
mounds hoard their bones as standing
stones of Avebury shade the shaggy goats.

And what of this mosaic Medusa unearthed
on the edges of a suburban Sussex neighborhood –
this palace yet another remnant of the lost world?

You dream of green rivers thick with boats.

Clouds and Eagles Fly By

There's a pale winter sun and
a crowded field of standing dead
cornstalks which shimmer and bend
in the wind, like beribboned arms
waving; golden husks of light in the end.
Fare well, old friend, fare well again.

Then One Day I Awakened

Then one day I awakened
and walked away from the paved road
after as many miles travelled
as to the moon and back.
And I named myself, oak.
Rooted. Strong hearted.
And I stood on the mountain.

There, I saw the violet, the pine
sapling, the blue face of rock,
the churned up river bending.
I saw how everything bends.
And I stood on the mountain
bowing, bowing in the wind.

Port St. Lucie, Florida

First light. A white feathered,
leggy chorus line strolls
across the suburban streetscape.
See concrete, double-wides, asphalt,
a little man-made lake, then
you're eye to eye with tenacious beauty –
these three whooping cranes –
red-faced and looming at the edge
of your father's front yard.
And this is the part where
soul swings open. Just like that
there you are and what matters
is what happens. The sun glows
like the last orange left in an old
grove, then bursts above the rooftops.

Laughing Gull

When we were kids, we
named every sea gull, "Joey."
Rocking in our little boat,
in the middle of the choppy bay,
we'd say, "Here's Joey, again."
Then hovering above us like a saint,
Joey would laugh. Everyone was happy.
The sea, green and deep enough.
The shimmering fish, biting.

Recess

Today, after a fierce game of kickball, I climbed
a ladder to retrieve a shoe from the school's roof.
I was not a witness to the arc and the spin of it.
I did not see the astonished faces – eyes skyward,
of the defending team. No.

I saw, instead, pale winter light and blue
mountains in silhouette like great sleeping
bears nestled around the schoolyard; then
a blue mountain reflected in a puddle of rain
on that flat roof – where one wayward shoe splashed down
and when, surely, the dream-deep mountain shuddered.

Angelical

Roger, the nine-year-old Romantic Poet, says,
"Her beauty interrupts me every hour."
Wordsworth and Keats, listen and weep.

Standing water in the ditch.
Articulate fritillaries lift and flit
adrift on the green golden air
like literate drunken sailors.

Fog. Sound of sea pummeling stony
cliffs of Cape Saint Mary's.
I wanted to tell you how
the thick mists parted and there,
rising from the choppy grey swell,
a stone island alive with gannets.
Some, their white necks outstretched,
point heavenward. And all the while
their guttural cries, their beaks intimately
clashing, their bows and great wings spread.
How they swoop in and alight.

Snail Trail

From inside my summerdark
house – half underground,
see gray day through
thick forest; this window
eye-level with blue spiderwort
where one undulant muscle,
beneath a spiral shell, glides
and ascends a bending green blade.

Ten years ago, in the Bronx
hospice hospital near Pelham Bay,
my mother chose the day
of her death. She said,
"I'm letting go now."

And I say grief is a tyrant.

Imagine walking on one foot
your home on your back.
Follow the sticky yet slick
and silver snail trail. See
how it dries to sparkle.
Grace notes on window pane.

And I say oh nautilus, fairy cup,
millennial mollusk, traveller, take your time.

Worthy

Open wide the mind's caged door.

−John Keats

Let's be honest, whispers

the blue-eyed grass,

this dappled roadside,

this puddle of rain,

myriad insect incantations,

the mind's shutters blown open,

holy this hollow and yes,

all is worthy, says

the blue-eyed grass.

Again

Quickly. So that I may be
with you again, make mine
a shallow grave. Let my flesh
mingle with living things –
my soul scatter. Let me
travel with worms, become
the sated bird's sudden song.

Raised Catholic

Sundays when the hunters can't hunt
I get religion in the autumn woods –
traveling on my knees like a Mexico City
Guadalupe pilgrim over decomposing leaves.
Then two ravens, clearing throats, wing
through the pine and poplar tops,
through the conundrum of drizzle.
There's a scent of fallen fruit. So I touch
myself. I touch myself again.
Now all is said and done amen.

Wilderness

In the valley of the shadow
of life, be wild.
Be wilder still.
Not fight or flight.
Not falling but standing still
in love.
Bewilder the civilized.
Be wild. Be wilder still.

Untitled

Leaves come in.

See their varied shades of green.

My house so much darker now.

And who loves the dark

but the shades

gladly welcomed guests.

   Through this window, look.

Late April spring.

    Wild pink apple blossom spring. Off

    in the woods, a turkey

tom sings.

   Take the house

   I'll be out here

Where everything says blurts shouts alive

      alive

Born in the Bronx in 1957, **Lynn Martin** hitchhiked around the country after leaving New York, traveled in Mexico, joined the Twin Oaks commune in Virginia, bartended in New Orleans, and worked in construction in Boston and D.C. before  settling down in Nelson County, Virginia, where she lived for many years in a cabin in the mountains. While making a living as a carpenter, Martin earned a B.A. from Sweet Briar College, where she studied with Mary Oliver. She went on to earn a M.Ed. from Lynchburg College and became a very creative, effective, and much-loved special education teacher. She often performed her poetry with backup musicians (who were also her godsons). Free downloads of some of these performances are available on the tenderbuttons.com website. This is Martin's second book. She died in 2016.

Acknowledgments

Grateful acknowledgment is made to the editors and publishers of the following periodicals in which poems in this collection were first published, sometimes as different versions:

Appalachian Journal: "Now, in Late October, I Can See"; "The Next World"

Poetry East: "Vixen" (as "Harris Hollow"); "Needing 29 Windows and Looking for a Break, I Went to the Factory in Rocky Mount"; "Deadfish/Rockfish"; "Yesterday I Went Out Early Into the Woods"

Poetry Northwest: "Woodwork"; "Carolina Handler"; "Seeds"; "By the River"

Southern Poetry Review: "Shiver"

Spillway: "Port St. Lucie, Florida"

Scratching Against the Fabric (an anthology of international poets) Unbound/Content (2015): "Continental Drift"